Sun Stains

poems by

Callie Hitchcock

Finishing Line Press
Georgetown, Kentucky

Sun Stains

Publisher: Leah Huete de Maines

Editor: Christen Kincaid

Cover Art: Callie Hitchcock

Author Photo: Callie Hitchcock

Cover Design: Elizabeth Maines McCleavy

Order online: www.finishinglinepress.com
also available on amazon.com

Author inquiries and mail orders:
Finishing Line Press
PO Box 1626
Georgetown, Kentucky 40324
USA

❖

Bleeding lightening bolt of anxiety in the morning
Heat of the day smears itself on my consciousness
Sun stains my skin wine red
Skinless yearning
Alien air of the subway so still, its static charge

Acid treacly cologne makes me long for a man to touch
Neon blood orange sunset
Blameless moon

Yellow christmas lights sagged
under the big front window

the door was empty in the middle
we just stepped through
hunched
flip flops clacking
sticky beer floor

I drank until I blacked out
woke up
looked for the pieces of the phone
I smashed in the street

by the time I got home
all that was left was the piece of obsidian
we had found when we were exploring
the trees behind the Museum of Anthropological Studies
and I said obsidian
          obsidian
          obsidian
                    all the way home

My delusions have got me this far, why stop now?

YVR airport
coming back after Christmas break
I ran up to you
sweaty from anticipation
while the fluorescent lights
and jovial airport art installations
seemed to beam over us with
conciliatory approval

You hugged me
or more clutched me
perceptibly wincing
a little bit

my excitement splashed back onto me
and spilled onto the floor
and I wondered if I should get someone
to clean it up or if it would
blend in with the rain
from outside

California

The sun is a hot nail in the sky. I run through the streets, trip and fall and instead of blood there is glitter. I lick the pastel houses and they taste like cream and mint. A palm tree scoops me up in its soft leaves and shows me the city. The ocean is neon blue. My smile is a jeweled bracelet.

By night the moon is a jellyfish. Glowing. Do you love me? I ask. The little eyes of stars blink. The silky ribbon grass shuffles. Do you love me? My eyes are shiny blue gems. I cannot close them. I float in the warm pool of consciousness. I am tea leaves, steeping in life, the flickering fever dream.

blind date

i am excited about the blind date but i don't want to be over excited about the blind date so that i don't feel a vacuousness if it doesn't work out but i also don't want to act too nonchalant so the people that set it up think i don't want to do it and thus they won't continue earnestly in making the connection but i also don't want the people who are making the connection to realize that i am jumping out of my skin at this opportunity and have already imagined a medium-ly sizable mental catalogue of romantic imaginings of what our nascent love would look like and bloom into in a golden summer of sun, with the faint rub of grass, in a vertiginous marble of sea, earth, sky, sky, sky.

It is November 20th, 10:23 am. I am on the 22 bus to go to the downtown Chipotle on Robson street in Vancouver, British Columbia after a morning of disappointing sex. It is a 40 minute ride from my house to Chipotle, as Google Maps predicted.

The bus is silent except for a woman with purple wine hair talking to a baby that is not hers. "Welcome to Vancouver little one!"

The bus patrons look on into their day thoughts.

I get off the bus at the Robson and Howe stop next to a Victoria's Secret. In the window I see a mannequin with a bright red bra that has a big red bow on the back like a sexy present. I do not feel like a sexy present.

I walk by a Chapters and go inside. There is a table titled "Miss Millennial" and showcases the titles:
#GirlBoss
How to Build a Girl
Never Have I Ever: My life (SO FAR) Without a Date
Is Everyone Hanging Out Without Me?
The Daily Face: Makeup on the go
In My Shoes

I walk up to the poetry section and listen to a throaty cover of "Kiss the Girl" from the Little Mermaid. I look at Joan Didion's Slouching Towards Bethlehem.

I fall into California reveries for 3 minutes.

I walk out of Chapters and go to Chipotle.

I request, purchase, and eat a steak burrito with white rice, no beans, no salsa, sour cream, and guacamole.

I wait at the 22 bus stop to go home.

A young man comes up to me.

What are you reading?
It's called Brief Interviews With Hideous Men
Oh cool.
Yeah.
Well you seem pretty cool.
Thank you.
Do you want to go on a date some time?
No thank you.

The bus comes right at that last statement. I get on it. I pull a taut plum out of my backpack.

Chewing the plum, the skin tastes hot and red.

10/12

Not feeling loved is like dying the slowest death.

10/19

My body belongs to me.

Vancouver Echoes

i.

A man comes up to me at a nightclub in Gastown and says,
"I'm too sensitive for this place, I can't handle the rejection,"
and wanders back into the warm darkness.

ii.
At Georgia and Granville a homeless man sits next to the
Skytrain. Waves of pigeons whirl softly around him
as he holds a loaf of bread.

iii.
Sitting on the 49 the back of the seat says,
"I don't love you anymore." Through the window I see
the forest huddled together in the rain.

iv.
Two girls sit against a log on Jericho beach,
the sun a golden medallion of the day,
the yellow center of a blue flower.
"I really trust the people doing the film, and besides,
I just don't believe God would put me in a bad situation."
"Oh Lola, every time I see you it's like we never parted."

Faceless

I picked
a big chunk of skin
off my lips

It felt exhilarating
and painful

I cried hard
on my couch
that smells like
mold
in my apartment
that is too small

My fantasy projects
mightily resist
disassembling

Like breaking a
rib

The slide from anxious confusion
to nothingness
is wordless, uninteresting,
too human

The slide from hope
to anxious confusion, though,
swells with a teaming furor

I trudge
into the crisp unknown
again
with a mug of tea
and a faceless dream

Oblivion

Every day without love
feels unbearable

Sometimes I am
distracted
from this truth
but it lies underneath
everything
waiting for me

There's a 20 second
stretch
at the top of the
Williamsburg bridge
where the air
doesn't smell like exhaust
it is my only oblivion

Despite my careful
polling of reactions
harvested from my friends,
I made a weird response
to your text

I woke up at 6 am
responded to it
and went back to sleep

Biking over the bridge
later that morning
I thought
what a perfect
and reasonable explanation
of my experience

Later when I told
my friends the entrails
of my perfect text
to you they said,
each in their own way,
You didn't say that
did you?

Which only proves my suspicion
that I am an alien
not meant for love
or this world's offering
of intense human connection

I am from:
a dizzy sumer
an apricot tree
a warm body
          Soaking in the sun

I wish to be
in the jaws
of oblivion

I hate the cold in my bones

Seasons of light

i.

You
in the forest
the sun turning you on
like a light

little white stone
of my heart

ii.

The street lamp
glowing down on the pink
cherry blossoms,
the soft shards of
dreams

iii.

By morning
glittering frost
crunching our fate
we are alive

iv.

In the fog
the day glows
muting the silence

I fall asleep in its
uncertainty

When it finally comes
it will be simple

One day
I will wake up
and you will
be there

Today
I got fired from my job

And yesterday
I saw a guy that I
was flirting with
at a few parties
on a Vespa
with a girl
in a tube top
sitting behind him
on the back

Most days
I am a glowing orb

I radiate the heat
the sun
steadily pours
on me

this
is the sweetest
love

the sun and I
we both give
endlessly

until we are
filled with gold

The gaping maw of the moon
stood steadfast
trying to swallow the earth
whole

I waited
for many years
hoping it would

I heard someone
coming up the stairs
of my heart

it was pulsing
with the heat
of a summer night
and not
taking visitors

I am in an unromance
with life

the days are
white coral pieces
drying on speckled sand
in the unrelenting
gaze of time

the sun
stares at me
and the days
I have laid out before it
unblinking
unflagging
patient
enduring
answerless

I sit quietly
the breeze blows
in my ear
and lifts
pieces of my hair
glowing threads
of light

I close my eyes
I am warm
life is measureless
yet must be measured

I must fit the years
into boxes of meaning

I must find a purpose
or make one
what is it inside
someone that makes
them want to do
something?
that makes them
want to be great?

it used to be fear
and pride. now
I am less afraid
but more confused

fear is a world
where you know
the answers

Reality is more
complicated than
any of my worst
case scenarios

What do you do
when the world
is not bite sized
and laid out?

Freedom wanders
around my heart
lackadaisically

It needs a directive

I must throw myself
into many projects

I can't run from myself
I have to face the world
and hold it close
Go.

Callie Hitchcock is a writer, journalist, and graduate of the NYU journalism Master's degree for Cultural Reporting and Criticism. She has published writing in *The Believer, The New Republic, The Nation, Los Angeles Review of Books, Slate,* and elsewhere. She is the producer and host of the podcast Nonfiction with Callie Hitchcock where she interviews nonfiction authors, writers, and journalists. She lives in Brooklyn.

www.ingramcontent.com/pod-product-compliance
Lightning Source LLC
Chambersburg PA
CBHW022109080426
42734CB00009B/1531